SUICIDE SURVIVOR

WRITTEN BY JOY E. HITZTALER, MA, LMHC

Copyright © 2018 by Joy E. Hitztaler

All rights reserved. Any unauthorized reprint or use of this material is prohibited. No part of this book may be reproduced or transmitted in any form or by any means, electronic or mechanical, including photocopying recording, or by any information storage and retrieval system without express written permission from the author.

Disclaimer: While all attempts have been made to verify the accuracy of the information provided in this publication, the author assumes no responsibility for any errors or omissions. Should the reader face any untoward website difficulties, it is recommended that they seek out professional technical support to rectify the same. The author will not be held responsible for any repercussions beyond the scope of this book.

Suicide Survivor

Contents

Chapter 1 Am a Suicide Survivor…

Chapter 2 Coping with the Grief

Chapter 3 Relax Tools for Balanced Health

Chapter 4 Anxiety & Depression – Symptoms and Tools to Help

Chapter 5 Suicidal Ideation Prevention by Recognizing Symptoms

Chapter 6 My Story

Chapter 7 Hope in the Midst – God Is a Part of My Coping

Appendix I Relax Tools Instruction for Parents,

    Relax Tools for kids including pictures

Appendix II Journal Prompts and Writing Space for You to Express Your

    Thoughts

Resources

Additional resources are available from the author

About the Author

Chapter 1

I Am a Suicide Survivor....

It was July 2010, mid-afternoon, I was at the local shopping mall in the Verizon store inquiring about adding a separate phone line for my growing small business. I was planning an office move the following month, and generally enjoying the break in the middle of my work day. I was six months pregnant with our first child. It was a beautiful day.

Then I had a message from my dad. His message asked me to call him after work because something had happened with my brother, Nate. I could tell from the sound of his voice this was going to be bad news. I called back immediately. It was indeed horrible news. Tragically, Nate had taken his own life that morning.

Returning to work that afternoon was out of the question. Instead, I joined my family at my mom's house. We all were in shock. We could hardly focus on planning for the funeral services the upcoming weekend.

We talked about Nate's recent activities, wracking our brains to try to make sense of it. For the last couple months, he had been struggling with mononucleosis. He had felt too poorly to go to work or properly care for his 15-month-old son. Just one month before Nate was diagnosed clinically depressed. His doctor had prescribed a medication to treat the depression. He also saw a psychologist for one session of counseling.

Nate had given no indication of any plans to hurt himself. In fact, he had travel plans scheduled for the summer and fall that year; plans for the future are usually an indication a person is looking forward—certainly not thinking of ending it all. Yet only a couple weeks into his treatment for depression, he ended his life.

Nate's death was a shock to everyone who knew him. We would have had an easier time understanding his death if he had fallen while hiking or rock climbing, as he loved going on outdoor adventures. Nate was full of life and laughter. He was generous, loving, funny, and smart, and family was of utmost importance to him. He enjoyed learning, playing games, traveling, reading, and being a husband and dad. We knew he was struggling with depression, yet this--taking his own life--was shocking.

Nate's life, the person he was, is so much more than this description, I cannot do him justice here. He was loved, and he loved others fiercely.

Nate's story is but a single example of what happens to many people who come to this sad place: the end of themselves. They can see no way out but by death. Each person who has died by their own hands has a story all their own. Each person who has died by their own hands was a son or daughter, husband, wife, brother, sister, friend, mentor, world-changer. Each person who died left behind suicide survivors, for whom I have written this book.

Death of a loved one by suicide creates a unique grief in the survivors. It may not always be shocking, yet it comes with extreme pain. Survivors often have questions that go unanswered this side of heaven.

Writing is an excellent outlet for emotions. Writing can help identify, organize, and express emotions and thoughts. Emotions from trauma and other challenging situations can feel like they have control over you; writing about the events, emotions, and thoughts can help you feel like you regain control.

Some people choose to keep their writing for review later, others rip up or delete the writing when finished. Some people write letters that are sent, while others write letters never intended to be read by anyone but themselves. You decide what to do with your writing, I just encourage you to put effort into this therapeutic processing activity.

***Journal prompt 1: What is the story of your loved one? What kind of person were they? What did they stand for? What are some memories you have of them and with them? What emotions did you experience shortly following their passing? What emotions (if applicable) have you been experiencing as time passes?

(Turn to Appendix II for space to express your thoughts in writing.)

I did not realize how many people have experienced the suicide of a loved one until I began sharing my story about Nate's suicide. In fact, the rates of suicide are high enough that you probably do know or interact with other suicide survivors, maybe at work, church, around the neighborhood, in the grocery store, and so on. It is a topic we like to bring up in conversation because it is uncomfortable, sad, and difficult, but discussing it with people who also have felt that grief is therapeutic.

Chapter 2

Coping with the Grief

Some thoughts on recognizing the symptoms of grief and how to cope with it.

Coping with the grief of losing someone you love to suicide has similarities to coping with grief brought on by other losses. When something terrible happens to us, like losing a loved one to suicide, we may turn inward. We may not know what to think or do with our emotions. It can be difficult to reconcile reality with what was life just hours or days before…reality of the person who is now gone. The grief you may feel as a suicided survivor compounded by the sudden shock of it and the guilt you may feel for not preventing it.

One mistake many of us make is to think that we are alone. As I said before, each story is unique to individuals, but this does not mean you are alone. Most suicide survivors feel similar emotions when you have lost someone to suicide. It is therapeutic to share your story and express your feelings with someone who has had a similar experience. Also, it is helpful and healthy to be a support to someone else who is hurting.

Grief is a lifelong journey, an individual and unique process, a kind of accepting, and overall growth following a loss. Just as each person is different, every journey is different.

Though our experiences are different, the symptoms of grief are the same. The symptoms can look a lot like depression. Grief is caused by a loss. A person can experience grief not only when someone dies, but also over the loss of a job, a home, a relationship, family member (through divorce or a move) or even the loss of a dream or vision for one's life. There is no formula, right pattern, or right way to go through the grieving process; there is no set time frame in which one should be finished grieving.

When you experience grief due to the death of a loved one, you may feel guilty for going on with life. In these cases, it can be helpful to do some things to honor the loved one lost. Easy thing to do include:

- Writing a letter to the person.
- Preparing the person's favorite food.
- Doing an activity the loved one enjoyed.
- Supporting a cause the person believed in.

***Journal Prompt 2: What ideas do you have for activities to do in memory of your loved one? What were they into? What did they enjoy doing? Food they liked? Music? Any things you enjoyed together? It can be hard to do things without your loved one, think how they would be happy you continued to enjoy what you once did together.

(Turn to Appendix II for space to express your thoughts in writing.)

I have myself found comfort in doing things in memory of my loved ones. I feel as though their lives and spirits can live on through these activities, and it has helped in healing my heart. For example, every year my family meets at Mt. Rainier in memory of my brother Nate because it was one of his favorite places. I make his favorite dessert bar, too. Nate worked at an outdoor clothing and gear store called *Patagonia*. Every year I add a few *Patagonia* pieces to my wardrobe. While my brother probably had a wardrobe full of *Patagonia* attire, and wearing the clothing fills me with memories of him and his dedication to conservation. Knowing he would be pleased that I support the environmentally responsible company makes me feel good.

In a similar manner, I do things to celebrate the lives of others I have known and loved, too. For example, I make mud pies for the deceased son of a good friend. Why mud pies? He actually liked to eat dirt as a toddler, and I know he would love the idea, gummy worms and all. Another way I commemorate a loved one is with raspberries. We now grow raspberries on our property. While they are delicious and fun to have, raspberries are also something my step-dad grew and loved. Likewise, my memories of my mother-in-law live on through a few heart and cat trinkets I keep around my house. She gave me some of them, and some I picked up myself because I believe she would have enjoyed them. Likewise, our son keeps memories of his grandpa alive with some clothes and toy airplanes. His grandpa, my father-in-law, was a fighter pilot in the Air Force. I enjoy talking to our kids about their late grandparents, uncle, and friend. I want our kids to know who they were and look forward to seeing all our family in heaven one day.

Speaking of heaven, I should mention here that my relationship with God has made an enormous difference in my coping and healing process. In short, acceptance of God being God, in control, loving all the time (even when I hurt and do not understand why) and His desire to take what is awful and use it for good, brings me hope. I have hope for painless life in Heaven, but I also have hope that in this life on earth I can experience joy, fulfillment, and satisfaction, even though I hurt tremendously.

I choose to trust in who God is, even when I am not comfortable, or feeling good. In fact, the depth of my feelings of loss, grief, depression, anxiety, shock and trauma, has given me an entirely new perspective and appreciation for life, for health, relationships, beauty, and my daily life with family. I have hope as I see God using my experiences enabling me to help other people heal and gain hope for their lives.

You may want to reconnect with God, too. A healthy faith is important to your coping healing. Scientific research into the success of such programs as Alcoholics Anonymous (AA) credits belief in a higher power as the key ingredient. There really is power in belief.

***Journal Prompt 3: What are your thoughts on a higher power? God? The universe? What part of your life does your higher power have? Do you pray or talk to God? Do you make decisions by the values connected to your beliefs? Do you mediate? Do you practice affirmation or mantras?

Do you talk about your higher power? Do people know about the value you place on, or your lack of belief in a higher power? What do those people closest to you believe? Are they supportive of your beliefs? Have you personally witnessed or felt evidence of a higher power in your life? How?

(Turn to Appendix II for space to express your thoughts in writing.)

Whether you have a strong relationship with a higher power or not, you will cope with the grief better if you change your thought habits. It will take some work on your part. Thought habits, like any other habit we have, can be changed. The first step is recognizing a negative thought when it enters your mind. Stop it in its tracks.

Ask yourself how you can turn the thought into a positive one, and determine what constructive thoughts you can replace the old destructive thoughts with. It may sound simplistic. It takes intention and practice to change thoughts, to replace old with new. We humans love familiarity. We love routine. We are drawn to what we know. So, it takes purposeful intention to recognize and replace damaging thought patterns to help you change your perspective and achieve the happiness you desire.

Like all of us, I have these hurts and painful memories that do not ever go away completely. They linger in the background and sometimes move more to the foreground, and back again throughout any given day. I have learned to control my thought patterns. The pain now allows me to see more clearly the value and priority in people instead of things. I appreciate time, beauty, laughter, and life in ways I could not have understood without my excruciating experiences.

In changing my own thought habits, I have chosen to keep my expectations based in reality. I choose to find and to see the good that can come out of the bad, even horrible things. I choose to expect life to have its ups and downs. The tide of the ocean comes in and goes out, likewise I know that good times and bad come and go. Every moment, every thought, every present is what our lives are made of. Sometimes people attempt to get through the mundane to make it to the vacation, the better house, better car, better whatever…but a life is made up of all the small moments, all the thoughts.

In the work of changing your thought patterns, you should ask yourself, what did you gain by having the old thought pattern? Could you have done even better if you had a different attitude? Be honest with yourself.

***Journal Prompt 4: What impact has your debilitating thought life and related emotions had in your life? What have you gained as a result of your thought patterns?

(Turn to Appendix II for space to express your thoughts in writing.)

Rather than deal with the negative thought patterns, people often find a way to get around the issue and still function. This is simply a band-aid, and is not balanced or healthy in the long run. An example of how this does not help you cope is a client of mine. She was a passenger in a car accident. She held so tightly to the trauma of the accident that she refused to get her driver's license.

In working with her, she realized that because she did not have a driver's license she needed people to drive her places. This provided her with companionship when she went anywhere. She also gained the reinforced love that people had for her as they spent the time to drive her places.

Her trauma was real, and we worked through that. We also identified and dealt with the gains she found in continuing to live in the trauma.

This client ultimately took driver's education classes and was preparing to take the driving test for her license when I last had contact with her. She decided that she could still ask people to accompany her to places, but that it was not always necessary. We had also worked to improve her self-confidence, self-esteem and self-worth. In sum, once her thought patterns were transformed, she was able to cope with the trauma, and she could change her feelings and her life.

In addition to examining and changing your thoughts, reading therapeutic books and materials about grief can be helpful. It is also good to have an outlet for your feelings, so do talk about your grief with family, friends, and a professional counselor.

Grief that results from a loss of a loved one by suicide is more painful than words can describe. Additionally, suicide carries a stigma, in that people may think the person was crazy, selfish, took the easy way out, and similar notions. If you know someone who has taken his or her own life, you may even feel shame. I believe these thoughts and feelings stem from our inability to understand why a person would do such a thing.

I recall that after my brother's death, a cousin of mine asked me-what was wrong with our family when we were growing up? The answer is-there was nothing wrong with our family; we had fairly normal struggles that go along with divorce and dividing our family life between two homes. We were blessed to have two homes with loving parents. The choice my brother made to take his life was his own. We cannot blame anything or anyone else or ourselves for his death--he ultimately made his choice.

It still pains me to know that my brother was in such a dark place, such a self-loathing place to want out so badly. He left behind a beautiful wife and son, along with his brother, sisters, parents and friends. Nate had so much potential, so much life, so much vision and love…

People who have not experienced this depth of emotional pain (debilitating depression and suicide ideation) cannot fully empathize with it. Recognize that depression is a mental health issue. It is an illness; the depressed person is unhealthy and has skewed thinking.

A depressed and suicidal person sees no way out of their circumstances and problems except by death. One suicidal client of mine expressed it as her desire to "just die". She said that she knew people would be sad and miss her, but they would get over it. That is so far from the truth!

People do not easily or simply get over the loss of loved one. Rather, I believe that we work out how to get through it, to absorb it into our life stories and emotions, and so it all becomes part of us. My own experience as a suicide survivor serves as proof of that. I have never "gotten over" the death of my brother. I have simply learned to live with it.

As you work on changing your thought habits, try this proven activity to help you cope with experience of suicide of a loved one. It is a wonderful therapeutic project that I do with my younger clients, but it works well for everyone. I have each client make a paper heart by cutting it out of a piece of paper. We rip it up as we discuss what happened and the hurt each of us feels. Then we put the pieces back together again by gluing them onto a piece of cardstock.

We talk about our emotions and feelings, identify our strengths. As we talk, we decorate the mended hearts with glitter, feathers, and color. The new hearts that we create as we talk about our hurt, pain, and developing new learning tools, are far more beautiful than they were before. The children are proud of their hearts, and they are especially pleased with the work they do to heal. With adults I can simply explain the project to get similar results; it is such a powerful metaphor.

This project helps people to cope by seeing what growth can come from our hurt. This project also helps you to realize that you will eventually find the silver lining in the dark clouds if you try. Finding the positive does not invalidate or minimize the bad, it is just intentionally choosing to grow from the experience. We can all see beauty in life when we look for it, when we make the choice to see it and create it.

Another way to cope is to seek help. Reaching out for help can be very hard for some people to do. When grief is caused by the suicide of a loved one, talking about suicide is the best way to heal and maintain good health. Sharing our hearts shares the load of the emotions around the traumatic event. If you are someone who is consoling a grieving person, opening your heart can mitigate the grief by saving the person from feeling like a victim. By identifying and expressing your own experiences and emotions, others can see that they are not in this alone.

Common emotions people experience as part of the grieving process include:

- shock
- denial
- pain
- guilt
- anger

- shame
- despair
- disbelief
- hopeless
- stress
- sadness
- numbness
- rejection
- abandonment
- confusion
- self-blame
- depression
- anxiety
- loneliness

***Journal Prompt 5: What emotions do you recognize in yourself as you grieve your loved one? What does it mean for you to have these emotions; do you believe something about yourself as a result? Do you notice some emotions that were present right away and others that came with the passing of time? What emotions do you think other people expect from you? Have you been surprised by emotions you've had surrounding the death of your loved one to suicide? Do you feel bad about any of the emotions you have felt? Are you confused as to why you would feel the way you have? Some people are quick to label what they're feeling to be able to let others know how they are doing. This can be limiting. Take the time to consider the various emotions that are common to grieving.

(Turn to Appendix II for space to express your thoughts in writing.)

Perhaps the single best thing you can do for your grieving loved one is to listen as they express their emotions. Be a safe person to talk to, express feelings, share memories, and fears. Talk about whatever stirs your heart. Encourage expression through song, artwork, and working one of the relax tools (explained in the next section).

Another way people express and cope with their grief is by crying. Crying is healthy, normal, and healing. Take it one day at a time, sometimes one hour or minute at a time. Encourage a person who is grieving, by saying something like, "You can survive this, even though it may at times feel like you're too broken."

When a friend or loved one takes their own life you may feel as if something is unfinished; questions are left unanswered. In my experience, passage of time enabled me eventually to accept the fact that I will never know all the answers. This acceptance helps me to find peace although I am still grieving. Knowing all the answers, the whys of whatever has happened, would not change the outcome.

It is more effective to focus on growing and moving forward than looking back and asking why. The grieving person may not be able to do that for some period of months or longer. Suggest the person be patient and gentle with themselves and allow themselves to grieve. The grieving process is lifelong, though often more intense immediately following the loss.

Grief is unremitting; it does not suddenly end one day. It ebbs and flows, and can be overwhelming at times, feeling bigger internally than anything externally. It can be troublesome to the grieving person that others are going on with life as usual but your own life is forever changed.

If you are comforting someone who is grieving the loss of a loved one, explain to the grieving person that some interactions with people will be awkward. Recognize that people want to express their compassion and sympathy but do not know what to say. Remind the grieving person that people have good intentions, care, and don't mean to offend. In the grieving process our emotions are heightened and more sensitive, causing a negative filter for what others say to you. A simple, "I'm sorry for your loss," is the most comforting.

Frequently, a great way to help a grieving person is to do little things for them. Simple, practical things you can do include such tasks as fix meals, run shopping errands, and watch the children. Sometimes they appreciate having you just be there, willing to listen, not needing to talk, accepting them even when they aren't doing well.

Being with someone who is grieving and depressed can be very draining.

Most people would choose to be with people who are upbeat, positive, and fun to be with and talk to. In the grieving process a person doesn't always feel like they can be happy and upbeat. It is important for you to continue your support and be willing to spend time with the grieving person even when they are having a bad moment. Console them by encouraging them to try to let go of any feelings of guilt or regret and be thankful for the time they had together.

Try this image for managing grief. Imagine an ocean. Suggest that managing grief is like an ocean; if you try to deal with it all at once, you wouldn't survive, but taking things one wave at a time, you can handle it. Sometimes you will be knocked down, caught off guard, but you are able to get back up and stand firm again. If other friends or family members are affected by this loss, encourage them to spend time together talking, crying, or just being together.

When you help others (whether it is regarding grieving or just helping) it ultimately helps you. Helping others can take your mind off yourself and help put some of your energies into blessing someone else.

I find helping others to be a great way to manage my own grief. When our family dog passed away, I was heartbroken. I did not want to cry all day. Instead, I distracted myself by spending the day cooking and baking for a friend's family who were in need. This helped me to focus my energy on something positive and not wallow in sadness all day. It may take an Herculean effort to make yourself do it, but you will feel better once you do. Likewise, in the passing of my parents and my brother, as well as our best friend's son, counseling others in my practice was ultimately helpful to me. It got my mind off me, it helped others, and at times, it made me thankful for what other terrible things had not happened in my life.

Balance is another key to coping– allow yourself to grieve but choose to feel the other feelings too. It is okay to be happy and excited, and still be sad and grieving. Being happy and laughing is not disrespectful to the person you have lost. We often have more than one feeling at a time, yet it can seem a bit wrong to be laughing in the time following a death.

Everyone grieves differently. Allow grace and space as others may be grieving in ways different than you; remember that there is no right way.

Set boundaries and limits. Following a loss you will likely feel less up to going about your normal day at the normal pace. While I found it exhausting to be processing and feeling all the emotions I was having, it was more difficult and tiring to do the normal daily activities. I also had difficulty sleeping, often waking in the night and thinking immediately of my loved ones lost.

Realize that you cannot rush the grief process. Accept it as a season and look to find ways to grow and give. Find things that help you in your grief and employ the skills described in this book when you're struggling.

Some people find support groups helpful. There may be a group in your area and there are also online resources (see resources page). I have personally run grief groups and can attest that they are powerful in processing and working through grief. My dad ran a support group for a time in the town he lived after my brother died by suicide. I know this was a source of help and healing for him. He also has participated in campaigns to raise awareness and work for suicide prevention.

Encourage a grieving person to keep doing what they know and like to do, it is helpful in their recovery. The grieving person will have times when they feel life cannot really go on, and will question whether they can ever be happy, fulfilled, or whole-heartedly smile…but they can, and will again eventually. It is my prayer and hope that you will have the opportunity to pass along the hope you find to someone in need.

Chapter 3

Relax Tools for Balanced Health

I recommend practicing these relax tools daily so that in the event you need them in periods of high stress, worry, anxiety, pain, depression, anger, or grief, using them will be second-nature to you. Until then, you will likely find daily benefits as you take time to relax, take care of yourself, and pay attention to what you are feeling.

• Mindfulness – pay attention to what you see, hear, feel in this moment. Be present, and pay attention to your body.

• Slow, deep breaths - Breathe in the good, breathe out the bad - Make sure to breathe deeply, noticing how your stomach moves out and in.

• Visualize yourself in a favorite place, with a favorite person, doing something pleasant

• Listen to music or sing

• Play a game

• Read – a book, a magazine, online

- Read or recite Scripture that speaks to the situation or feelings you are having. Choose to believe God's truth over the lies the world would tell us.

- Watch a movie or show, listen to an audio clip – comedy is especially helpful as laughter changes your brain chemistry.

- Write or draw to express feelings

- Take a shower or bath – aromatherapy can be helpful too (oils, lotions, candle)

- Have a drink of water or tea; ask yourself if you're hungry as this can alter how you feel.

- Do an activity or exercise – work out the adrenaline, when upset your brain creates extra adrenaline for the fight or flight response. Exercise also creates feel-good chemicals in your brain.

- Lay down, take a nap. Lack of sleep changes everything.

- Get away to be by yourself. Everyone needs a time out sometimes!

• Talk with a friend, family member, or counselor (make a list of people you can trust and reach out to for support.)

• Recall how you've managed difficult times/problems in the past – is there something that can be applied again? Remind yourself that you made it through that other experience; you can make it through this one, too.

• Make a list of things you like to do. These can be good choices when you're upset.

• Make a list of things you're looking forward to, or your goals, ambitions, and values.

• Make a plan. Envision where you would like to be in terms of your relationships, work, home, finances, spiritual, creativity? Think this year, five, ten years and beyond. Then look to where you are now and explore what steps can come between now and your goals.

Relax Tools for kids involve the same principles, just presented in a fun way.

See Appendix I Relax Tools for children accompanied by instructions for parents.

***Journal Prompt 6

What Relax Tools do you think you use or would like to try? What do you enjoy doing? What activity can you do while being intentional to relax, calm down, center yourself? Remember to be thankful for this time, appreciative of your body and how you can have control.

(Turn to Appendix II for space to express your thoughts in writing.)

Chapter 4

Anxiety, Depression, & Suicidal Ideation (SI)

When you lose a loved one to suicide allow yourself time and space to grieve. Also, be aware of the ways that trauma and grief manifest themselves—anxiety and depression are common. Notice if you are having suicidal thoughts yourself, known as Suicidal Ideation (SI). You may not be aware that being close to someone who has taken their own life puts you at risk for considering self-harm as well.

In terms of suicide prevention, recognizing anxiety and depression in yourself or a loved one, and seeking help can decrease suicide rates.

Statistics show the majority of people who either attempt or complete suicide are depressed. Knowing that fact makes it easy to see that recognition and treatment of symptoms can decrease suicide rates.

How can you recognize anxiety? Watch for the following symptoms of **anxiety** disorders:

- Excessive, uncontrolled worrying most days for about six months.
- Feeling restless or hyperactive.
- Irritability.
- Tiring easily.
- Experiencing muscle tension/tightness.
- Difficulty concentrating.
- Trouble sleeping (to include falling asleep and going back to

sleep).

If you notice symptoms of anxiety, what can be done to alleviate it?

A variety of techniques can help, and I have compiled several that I have found to be most successful for my clients. You can find them in the "Relax Tools" section of this book. Practice different ones to determine which of them work best for you or your loved one.

An important step in managing your anxiety is to identify any upsetting memories, events, or emotions that may be causing it. Try to identify a memory or event that triggered the anxiety, perhaps it set off a panic attack or very anxious feelings. This indicates that you need to do some processing and healing around that triggering event or item. It is a good idea to talk with your doctor and a professional counselor.

Depression is another emotion associated with grief. How can you recognize depression? Symptoms of **depression** include:

- sleeping more than normal or less than normal.
- loss of motivation and interest in activity previously interested in.
- increased irritability.
- marked increase in anger or rage.
- anxiety.
- feelings of hopelessness and despair.
- difficulty concentrating.
- change in a person's work/school performance.
- change in eating habits.
- noticeable carelessness or neglect of grooming habits—no

longer caring about their appearance or housekeeping.
- frequent absence from school/work, and they may often complain about feeling sick.
- participation in discussions about death or suicide, in person or online.
- creating poetry and artwork around death.
- self-harm.

If you are having several of these symptoms for more than several days, talk with someone soon. If someone you know or love is showing these symptoms, let them know you care, and ask if you can help. Try to determine if they are willing to get professional help.

In thinking about depression, imagine it as existing on a continuum. At the milder end of the continuum is dysthymia (persistent feelings of sadness, being down). Moving along the continuum to about mid-range you can find mood disorder, then depression, bipolar disorder and finally major depressive disorder at the extreme end. Just as every single person is different, diagnosis and effective treatments for depression vary as well. Known parameters exist for accurate diagnosis (found in a widely used reference book called, *The Diagnostic Statistical Manual for Mental Health*) and the effective relief of the symptoms of depression, and ultimately healing.

Of all of the symptoms of depression listed above, the last one—self-harm-is of particular concern. People who self-harm by cutting and other self-harming actions are not usually intending to kill. Nonetheless, it is serious because sometimes self-harming can lead to accidental death. Self-harming behaviors can be treated with professional help.

Self-harming behavior is similar to addiction. The individual often has deep pain underlying the behavior. They derive some degree of relief from self-harm. Focused talk therapy or counseling can assist the individual in digging up, processing, and working to heal emotional wounds. Also, through counseling, the person can learn skills to better cope with pain.

Sometimes, people can self-treat by reading therapeutic material, or talking with family, friends, pastors, therapists, or other individuals who can offer support, and bring themselves through the healing process. Add to it professional counseling, which can be a wonderful way to keep the self-treatment progressing and staying on course to recovery. As a counselor myself who has benefited from counseling, I have experienced firsthand the benefits of professional help. I now consider myself blessed to be able to help other people in their healing and growth.

Professional counseling is very important in treating depression. Trying to self-treat depression on your own can take longer and be less successful. Depression can be extremely challenging to manage without professional counseling. One type of depression particularly worth discussing here is Bipolar disorder.

A person with Bipolar disorder has alternating episodes of depression and mania. Mania will cause problems at work, school, and in relationships. In the manic phase, the person is highly distractible. Other symptoms of mania are: lacking need for sleep, unusually rapid speech or motor activity, talking excessively, and discussing grandiose ideas and beliefs about themselves that are not realistic. A manic person also tends to be involved in risky activities or behaviors such as huge purchases, gambling, and irresponsible sexual behavior.

If you or a loved one shows signs of depression, what can you do to alleviate it? The best way to begin to alleviate depression is to talk to someone--family, friends, and/or a counselor. You should check the "Relax Tools" section of this book for a list of techniques that you may find helpful.

Whichever techniques you try, do not bury emotions and memories that are difficult. It is these very memories and emotions that you need to finish processing and expressing so healing can happen. Healing takes time and effort on your part. Meanwhile, try to do what you generally do—keep to your routines and activities--even though you may not feel like it. Pay attention to your eating and sleeping habits; they are vital to health and balance. Make time for exercise, even just walking. Exercise of any kind creates feel-good chemicals in the brain. You should also discuss your symptoms with your doctor, in addition to a mental health counselor.

Chapter 5

Suicidal Ideation and Prevention

Suicidal Ideation (SI), or plans around how to end one's life, is alarming. For some people, the grief is too much to bear and the idea of ending the pain sounds good. Even when they experience the trauma, pain, and loss of a loved one to suicide, ending their own lives can be appealing. When the pain becomes too much to bear, suicide may seem a viable solution. But rational, healthy thinkers know that suicide is not the solution to any problem.

You may have already noted that depression, anxiety, grief and SI share some common symptoms. Of all the symptoms of depression, SI is of paramount concern. Planning shows the depth of the person's thinking about suicide as an option.

If you discover a loved one is planning suicide, explain to the person that suicide is not the answer. Professional help is needed immediately, and a trip to the hospital emergency room may even be warranted.

Once the urgency is passed, you should continue to talk to the person about the fact that suicide is not the answer for a while longer. Once a person has considered suicide, they will likely think about it again. A person with SI is rather like an alcoholic—even when an alcoholic remains clean and sober, the risk for relapse remains. Even as a suicidal person regains hope in life, there will be times when things are stressful, difficult, painful, and seeming hopeless.

Keep communication open with a person who has had suicidal ideations. Do not worry that you may replant the suicidal thoughts. Bringing up the topic is beneficial because conversation will let the person express the painful emotions can help alleviate the pain.

If you yourself are feeling like you want to die, or thinking about how to end your life, please ask for help immediately. Suicide is not the solution to your problem. Call the crisis line 1-800-273-8255, go to the hospital, or just tell someone you are feeling this way. You are valuable and there is help for you.

If you are a parent with a teenage who is suffering with depression, be aware that depression is the leading cause of teen suicide, despite the fact that depression is very treatable. According to research, about 75 percent of suicides or suicide attempts are completed by people suffering from depression. This fact means that by treating depression, we can decrease suicide rates.

We all need to learn to recognize symptoms of suicidal ideation. When we can recognize symptoms, there is a chance to help the people hurting.

When a person cannot see any way other than suicide out of a situation, that person feels stuck in a place of deep pain and sees no hope. Once a person considers suicide as an option, the person often continues to see it as an option. In this mental state of SI, it is important to have a couple of people to talk to.

Once a person gets past the immediate SI, the person is still at risk. This person needs to be reminded often that hope exists, feel supported, and be reminded that suicide ultimately will not solve the problem the person may be having.

SI often occurs in people with some form of mental illness, anxiety, depression, and/or substance abuse issues. Substance abuse itself may be a sign the person is struggling with emotional or mental distress. Substance use is a way for someone who is struggling and uncomfortable to feel better.

Substance use offers only a momentary escape, distraction, and numbs the pain the person is feeling. But it is a quick fix, a self-medicating solution that lasts only for a short time. Once the effects wear off the user is left with the same hopelessness and pain. The best solution is for the user to deal with the painful emotions through professional counseling and get back on the path to a healthy, happy life. This is a better solution than death.

People in this state of distress, feeling suicidal, may not reach out for help themselves, but often their family and friends can spot the signs. Here is a list of the warning signs you may see exhibited by a person struggling with depression and **SI**:

- change in their normal behavior.
- new behaviors, such as increased use of drugs or alcohol.
- behaving recklessly.
- isolating themselves, involved less with people.
- sleeping more than normal or less than normal.
- visiting and saying goodbye to people.

- giving away possessions.
- Uncharacteristic aggression.

In conversation with a person who is depressed or suicidal, take note if they talk about:

- being a burden.
- being trapped.
- having unbearable pain.
- having no reason to live.
- commenting that no one cares about them.

Sometimes people talk about the desire to hurt or kill themselves. Take these statements seriously.

If you are with or know of a person having suicidal thoughts, you need to get **professional help immediately**. You have some options:

1. Call 911 and ask for a wellness check for someone who is suicidal. A police officer will visit and have a conversation with the person. If the person cannot make statements about staying safe, he or she will be taken to the hospital where their safety can be assured.

2. You may want to take the person to the hospital emergency room, or to their doctor or walk-in clinic.

3. Call a suicide help line with the person (National Suicide Prevention Lifeline: 1-800-273-TALK (8255)

Whatever you do, do not leave them alone. If possible, remove any weapons, alcohol, drugs, or sharp objects that they could use to harm themselves.

Be aware that certain conditions **make the risk of suicide higher** than normal. These include:

- Previous suicide attempts.
- History of family suicide or attempts.
- Stressful events (i.e. divorce, loss of job, loss of house, severed relationship, trouble in school or major friend drama).
- Prolonged stress.
- Access to realistic means of hurting or killing oneself.
- Mental health conditions.
- Other risk factors such as the person has witnessed a suicide or violent act, or has fought with or bullied a person who died.

Some circumstances are risk factors **specific to teenagers,** especially those already dealing with depression. They include:

- their parent's divorce.
- domestic violence in the home.
- struggle with grades.

- rejection or bullying by peers.
- death of someone they know (even a friend they know only through online interaction).

Again, take seriously any talk centered on suicide and thoughts of death. If someone talks about suicide, you should not treat it casually or disregard it. I often suggest to clients that people who talk about suicide be taken to the emergency room to show them the seriousness of their statements.

Sometimes a teen repeatedly threatens suicide as a manipulation strategy to get attention and get their way. Having a parental relationship with a child who repeatedly threatens suicide is very stressful. Their threats may be an attempt to express their extreme pain, hurt, confusion, and need for help. On the other hand, such SI can also be serious planning that ultimately will be carried out. Such thinking is often a result of depression.

I should point out that some people have chemical imbalances that cause depression, and they can also have depression brought on by a specific situation. Some people struggle for years with depression and suicidal thoughts. People who battle depression for many years may not have specific reasons or experiences to explain their depression; their brains have a chemical imbalance. Depression due to a physiological condition such as this is still a serious condition, one that is very real to people with this condition, and they need professional help.

According to research and my own experiences with my clients, medication combined with counseling, is the most successful treatment for depression caused by a physiological rather than emotional condition.

This is how I take part in Suicide Prevention, and I invite others to join.

As a mental health counselor, I have the honor of walking alongside people as they process through grief, loss, anxiety, depression, and SI. Not only those involved in the mental health field can help; **everyone can take part in prevention when we recognize the signs and love people enough to say something.**

Training for people of all ages and understanding their roles in recognizing symptoms (described in previous sections) of depression, anxiety, and suicidality can help prevent suicides. When people recognize symptoms, they can ask for help, offer help, and encourage others to get help.

Resilience can be defined as the ability to cope with adversity and to adapt to change. Resilience is a protective factor against suicide risk. Part of being resilient includes an attitude of optimism, having hope, and having a positive self-concept.

In kids, two factors have been found to determine resiliency: individual personality and relationship with a consistent adult that is a healthy example.

Encourage social connectedness for your children and loved ones. We all need support, we were created for community. Sometimes we need help and other times we are the one helping. Some messages from society push individualism, comparison, competitiveness, but these are not the healthiest.

Hope makes all the difference. Hope pulls a person up when they've fallen, gives perspective to life, and hope can peel a person's body out of bed to face another day. Hope can alter perspective from barely surviving the waves, to enjoying the surf, jumping, playing, learning, growing, and facing the challenge of life head-on.

Hebrews 6:19 says, "This hope we have as an anchor of the soul, both sure and steadfast…"

Client Feedback – What helps when you're feeling suicidal?

I gathered these tidbits from conversations in my counseling sessions with teens and adults who were suicidal. This is the feedback I received when I asked the client about what would help, when someone is suicidal. Much of it is insightful.

- People don't like the cliché, "It will be ok", whatever the problem, it is real and huge to them.

- Encourage the idea that tough times make you stronger; they help you to see how tough you really are. People say they just want to give up. Things are too hard.

- Teenagers are doing things they shouldn't be at their young age – sex, drugs, have weapons. Some think there is something wrong with them. Teenagers told me school is worse now, the bullying, rudeness, judgmental people, and it's as though there is no filter for people's words, especially with all the technology.

- Home life is what can cause suicidal thoughts – it's hard to talk to someone when things are hard at home, hard to seek professional help, and it may not be common to see the counselor at school (they do more scheduling and other duties aside from giving counsel).

- Teens tell me they don't want to talk with someone they don't know. All ages say they feel like a burden to those around them. I even had an elderly lady tell me that people would mourn her loss for a little while, but they would get over it...this is just not true.

- People tell me that hope came when they were able to talk about it all.

If you or someone you know has something to add, something to ask, please e-mail me at joy@joyhitztaler.com Community is stronger, we all learn from each other. Love is strongest.

Chapter 6

My Story

I want to share with you my own life story to help you realize that I do understand your suffering. You read the part of my story of being a suicide survivor; this is the bigger picture of my story. We can all find the academic knowledge we seek in textbooks, classes, or even the internet. In my view, however, one of the best sources of knowledge is simply what we learn from our life experiences and from sharing them with other survivors.

I consider myself blessed now because throughout my own journey in adulthood, I have been able to use my formal training and experience in helping friends and family on many occasions, and myself as well. In fact, I have wondered whether it is my clients or myself who have benefited more from my education in counseling.

My own story--my life--has been filled with many wounds. Like so many of us these days, I struggled as a young kid with my parent's divorce. Around the same time as the divorce, I was sexually abused by a family member. I prayed, and I asked God to help me forget it, but I did not seek counseling or tell anyone about the experience for another ten years. We do not always understand why such things happen. Through the prism of time, however, I found at least one silver lining in these traumatic childhood experiences: they have enabled me to be a better counselor.

I understand what a child feels when parents' divorce. As prevalent as divorce is, my own childhood suffering over my own parents' divorce allows me to better connect with clients who have had a similar experience, both children and adults. Sexual assault in one form or another is more common than many people know. Coping with sexual assault is especially difficult for children and women who were victims of it. My personal experience as a victim allows me to empathize with other victims, children and adults, in ways others cannot.

Depression is another affliction that I have struggled with a handful of times. My first memory of it is during my junior high school years. I had begun working with a counselor after having trouble at school with sexual harassment. That experience, combined with my vivid memory of my childhood sexual abuse--that I had not yet dealt with--led me finally to see a counselor.

I also recall telling my mother that I didn't know if I wanted to live, I just hurt so much. She calmly reminded me of all the people who loved me and advised me that things will heal in time. I recall also talking with my dad, who himself has struggled with depression. At one point he was hospitalized because of his suicidal thoughts. I should note that it is common for mental health struggles to affect multiple generations in families. What I was feeling was the result of my experiences and my genetic tendencies.

Deeper depression plagued me in my college years. I had gone on a mission trip to Africa and returned with intestinal parasites. Recovery took three years, several specialists, and a naturopath. Finally, I returned to a healthy and normal life and diet. During the years I was sick, I became deeply depressed. I became angry at God for allowing me to get so sick while I was out telling people about Him. Fortunately, God is patient and can handle my anger along with whatever I feel and tell Him.

As a college student working with a youth group, I realized I needed further counseling regarding my molestation. It was during this counseling work that I decided I wanted to become a counselor myself. I wanted to impart hope in others and aid in their healing. I knew that I had found my life purpose when I graduated college with a degree in psychology and then obtained my master's degree in counseling psychology.

After all that, I entered the world of adulthood: got married, bought a home, started my private practice. Before long, however, I found myself depressed again. By now I knew that counseling was helpful. I began another round of counseling and taking an antidepressant. Adding to my stress, my husband and I were going through a difficult period with our parents. One of my parents was fighting cancer, and both of my in-laws were dealing with cancer and multiple strokes. The three of them passed away in the same two-year time frame.

Then my brother became clinically depressed. He started medication, and to everyone's great shock, he took his own life. Less than one year later while on a camping trip with our best friends, their beloved son drowned in a tragic accident. As you can imagine, five deaths in just two years left us reeling. We had not dealt with one loss before another one came.

After so much loss, I decided to see a counselor again to be sure I was as healthy as I could be dealing with all the tragedy. I wanted to be able to do my job well. I am thankful that I had then, and have now, the skills of a counselor to deal with all the hurt in my life.

Near the end of that tragic two years, God blessed us. We had our first child. Our daughter was indeed a gift of life, a gift of incredible motivation, joy, and love. Our family continued to grow. Following our third child, I suffered from post-partum depression (PPD). Different from the other bouts of depression, PPD took me a little while to recognize. I again began medication to assist in balancing my hormones that had gotten wacky following birth, nursing, and the process of weaning my one-year old son.

I now have a fairly typical life, managing all of the different roles adult women have: wife, mom, friend, daughter, sister, career woman and business owner (private practice counselor). Like most people, my relationship stress, financial stress, and daily living stressors cause ups and downs. I have numerous family and friends who have themselves struggled with SI, depression, anxiety, and grief. I imagine you, also, have people in your life struggling with these symptoms, and possibly, this is where you are right now. I hope and pray that this information is helpful for you and your loved ones as you tread the waters of suicide survival.

Chapter 7

Hope in the Midst

Personally, my faith in God and my relationship with Him is a vital foundation for my life. Even if you do not believe or trust in God, maybe you are unsure what to think, read on in case you find something valuable.

We choose what to focus on – make the choice to look to God.

• Col. 3:2 "Set your mind on things above, not on things on the earth."

• Rom. 8:5 "For those who live according to the flesh set their minds on the things of the flesh, but those who live according to the Spirit, the things of the Spirit. "

• Psalms 94:18, 19 says, "If I say, "My foot slips,' your mercy, O Lord, will hold me up. In the multitude of my anxieties, within me, Your comforts delight my soul."

• Isaiah 41:10 says, "Fear not for I am with you. Be not dismayed for I am your God. I will strengthen you, I will help you. I will uphold you with my righteous right hand."

- I Peter 5:6, 7 says, "Cast all your anxiety on Him because He cares for you."

- "There is no fear in love. But perfect love drives out fear, because fear has to do with punishment. The one who fears is not made perfect in love." John 4:18

- 2 Timothy 1:7 says, "For God gave us a spirit not of fear but of power and love and self-control (sound mind)."

- Four G's – when I live believing these truths, I will feel the freedom of the finished work of Christ.
  - God is great so I do not have to be in control (Psalm 27)
  - God is good so I do not have to look elsewhere for satisfaction. (Psalm 94)
  - God is glorious so I do not have to fear others. (Psalm 31)
  - God is gracious so I do not need to prove myself to anyone. (Psalm 103, Luke 15:11-24)

God promises closeness to those who mourn.

- Matt. 5:4 "Blessed are those who mourn, For they shall be comforted."

- Job 5:11 "He sets on high those who are lowly, And those who mourn are lifted to safety."

- Isaiah 61:3 "To console those who mourn in Zion, To give them beauty for ashes, The oil of joy for mourning, The garment of praise for the spirit of heaviness; That they may be called trees of righteousness, The planting of the Lord, that He may be glorified."

- In John chapter 11 Lazarus has died and Jesus weeps with Mary in her pain and loss, even though He knows that's not the end, He would raise Lazarus to life again. Jesus wept with his friend. Jesus grieved the loss of his friend, even though He knew what was to come.

- Ann Voskamp says, "I can sing because I know *what* is coming. I can hope because I know *who* is coming. Psalm 34:18-19.

- Real hope is not rooted in the absence of pain, suffering and heartache.

- John 11:6 says, "Jesus loved Martha and her sister and Lazarus. So when He heard that Lazarus was sick, He stayed where he was two more days." Ann Voskamp notes, "*So*. He loved them and so He didn't move immediately…He loves me and *SO* He allows me to feel pain that draws me to Him." This is a hard concept to accept. Hard to think about and see that ultimately the hard is good.

- He is our hope for life, not only our hope for Heaven someday, but our hope for today too. John 10:10 says, "The thief does not come except to steal, and to kill, and to destroy. I have come that they may have life, and that they may have it more abundantly."

- Jesus says in Mark 8:34, "Don't run from suffering: embrace it. Follow me and I'll show you how. Self-help is no help at all. Self-sacrifice is the way, my way, to saving yourself, your true self."

- God asks us to trust more in who He is, and not so much on what He does i.e. what happens. This is so very hard to live out! Daniel 2:17-18 says, "…But even if He (God) does not (save us) …" (we will follow Him and not worship another.)

- Feelings will come and go, "Jesus Christ is the same yesterday, today, and forever." Hebrews 13:8 God loves us all with a love that does not change, regardless of our position/circumstance.

- Ravi Zacharias notes that sermons, no matter how sincere, cannot answer the unsolvable problems. "Rather, together with the Spirit the sermon exists to point out that having answers is not essential to living. What is essential is the sense of God's presence during dark seasons of questioning. Our need for specific answers is dissolved in the greater issues of the Lordship of Christ over all questions – those that have answers and those that don't."

- II Corinthians 3:17 "Now the Lord is the Spirit and where the Spirit of the Lord is there is Freedom."

- Our children are God's, entrusted to us for a time. We can choose to replace our fear with God's promises.

- God promises to put His laws on the hearts and minds of his children. Hebrews 8:10-11

- God knows how to finish the good work that He has started. Jeremiah 29:11 & Philippians 1:6

- God loves our children even more than we do as parents. John 3:16, Romans 5:8, Ephesians 2:4-5.

- Faith requires trust, giving up control. Work to make your FAITH be bigger than your FEAR. John 16:27 says, "In this world you will have many troubles, fear not, I have overcome the world."

- 1 Corinthians 13:13 says, "Three things will last forever—faith, hope, and love." Faith, hope and love are present now and will be present in heaven too, they last forever.

- Joyful confidence in God. *Joyful.* II Corinthians 7:16 "Therefore I rejoice that I have confidence in you in everything." Joyful confidence that God is good, even when things do not feel good or seem good in our way of understanding. Joyful by definition is not dependent on circumstances, as happiness is. Joy comes from inside, happy comes from outside.

- We need to pray for our children, that their soul be secure in the hope and confidence only Christ gives.

- These hard times are pressing us and enabling us to produce God's fruit.

- Philippians 3:13-14 "But one thing I do: forgetting what is behind and straining towards what is ahead, I press on towards the goal to win the prize for which God has called me heavenward in Christ Jesus."

- Hebrews 6:19 "We have this certain hope, like a strong unbreakable anchor holding our souls to God himself."

- Matthew 5:4 "Blessed are those who mourn, For they shall be comforted." This verse is a part of a list of several instances in which Jesus was telling people they were blessed, had reason to rejoice and be thankful. For some time, I could not see the blessed part of mourning! It hurt so badly, how can that be blessed? Loss and heartache, how can that be blessed? Gaining a thankfulness, a thanks-living perspective, appreciating people and life and beauty. That is a blessed part of mourning.

Above all Jesus was telling us that we are blessed when we mourn because He comforts us. The God of the universe, who created everything, loves us so much more than we can imagine, and He comforts us, comes near to us when we mourn. It is so blessed to be near to Jesus that even mourning can be blessed as it draws us near, it links our hearts with His.

If you do not Know God and that He loves you unconditionally, you can pray the prayer below. I recommend following it up by reaching out to local supports--people who know and love Jesus. Feel free to e-mail me with questions, and I'll do my best to find an answer and connect you with others joy@joyhitztaler.com

God, I know that I am a sinner (all have sinned Romans 3:23). Please forgive me of my sins and wash (forgive me I John 1:9) me clean. I accept (believe John 16:24) your son Jesus and pray (for salvation John 16:24) that He will come to live in my heart. Thank you for saving me.

Look up the Scriptures noted in this prayer. If you do not have a Bible, there is a great app for your phone called "You Version" and the same company has a website www.youversion.com You can search key words, topics, and find studies there.

Anyone and everyone can be involved in the prevention of suicide. As you've read through this book, you've learned the warning signs and symptoms of depression, now it's your turn to tell others so they can learn and help too!

Appendix I

Relax Tools Instruction for Parents

Practice a few of these tools each day. Find some that are your favorites and that seem to work the best in calming your child down. Many of these tools help to interrupt the flow of upsetting emotions. Some of them distract. In talking about the issue the child was upset about, it is ok to take a break to allow emotions to calm down. Revisiting the issue later will be more productive in terms of finding a compromise or solution.

*Slow breaths – It can be helpful to breathe in, say "Mississippi" or "hippopotamus" then breathe out, next number.

*Blow bubbles – practice blowing softly like you are blowing real bubbles, so they would not pop.

*Be like a turtle – Everyone needs a time out, even turtles draw themselves into their shells. Suggest your children recognize and take time to themselves when they need to.

*Do some exercise – when we are upset our bodies create extra adrenaline as part of the fight or flight response. It can be helpful to exercise to use up the extra adrenaline. Exercise also creates feel-good chemicals in the brain.

*Play a game -sometimes diversion or distraction is helpful. Doing an activity we enjoy will help calm and create feel-good chemicals in the brain.

*Visualize your favorite place – by thinking of a favorite place, person or activity it helps to calm down. It can help to distract from the upsetting issue.

*Find Scripture that speaks to the issue going on. For example, in struggling with worry one could keep in mind, Isaiah 26:3 "You will keep him in perfect peace, Whose mind is stayed on You, Because he trusts in you." This can also work using mantras or other sayings.

*Pray, meditate – this is self-explanatory. Taking time to relax and express your mind and heart is healthy venting.

*Talk to someone – venting and sharing the burden of feelings can be helpful.

*Have something to drink – drinking something like water, milk, or juice, forces the body to calm down as breathing and the heart beat slow down.

*What ideas do you have? Doing activities we enjoy helps to balance us, calm us, and make good-feeling chemicals. Ask your kids to come up with ideas of their own to relax or vent.

*Be like a raw noodle and then a cooked noodle – Raw noodles are stiff, suggest a stiffening and flexing of the entire body, then a release and relaxing of all the body. Sometimes we don't realize where we are tense and tightening muscles, so flexing and then relaxing is great.

*Write or draw what you're feeling – venting in art and writing is very helpful. We identify feelings to write about them or draw to express them. We do not always think in full sentences. Writing down our thoughts forces us to process them more completely. Color can also be powerful to assign to various feelings.

*Read some jokes, watch something funny – laughing changes the chemistry of your brain, it creates feel-good chemicals, dopamine and serotonin.

*Read – this can help to distract us from what is going on in the present. It can allow time for emotions to calm down, as well as give the mind a rest from thinking of the upsetting issues. If you read to learn something new, reading can be a positive focus of time, energy and focus.

*Watch a show – this is a distraction, giving time to calm down. The break can also give the mind a rest from thinking about the upsetting issue and allow emotions to lower.

*Helping someone else – gets our minds off ourselves (and the upsetting issues) and onto someone else. It is a distraction as well as a perspective-gaining opportunity. Helping can bring value and appreciation, awareness of talents and skills.

*Pop a balloon or rip paper – sometimes destruction and noise feel good when we're upset. Maybe recycling or scrap paper can be an option to rip up.

*Shake the Dog or do the wiggle – like a dog shakes off when wet, or shaking out your hand when it's tired from writing a bunch, shaking your body relaxes tense muscles. It also feels silly and often causes us to smile or laugh.

*Squeeze a stress ball – this exerts energy that feels to be at an overflowing amount when upset. It is also very transportable, a tool that can be employed in many locations appropriately.

*Sing or listen to music – music is powerful in mood-setting. It can help get our mind off upsetting issues as well as just calm down our emotions.

*Take a nap – sometimes after some rest we think more clearly. Sleep can be a distraction and break from upset feelings and thoughts.

*Take a shower or bath – relaxing in a shower or bath can help calm emotions down so that we can better problem solve, keep going with daily responsibilities, or compromise.

*Consider changing your thoughts – for example, the dentist is a crummy thing we always have to do. Change this to, going to the dentist is a necessary helpful, healthy thing we do to take care of our bodies, and (for kids) you even get a new toothbrush and a prize after being a good patient.

*Tell your negative thoughts and worries to go away. For example, we might think, "I'm afraid I will fail the upcoming test." Instead, tell yourself, "I am not going to think that way! I'm nervous about the test but last time I did fine, and there's no reason I won't do okay this time, too." If your kids are stressing about something, suggest that they act out kicking the negative emotion. Soon, they will be having fun and more relaxed.

*Breathe in positive and breathe out negative thoughts. Try to encourage keeping thoughts simple and picturing good things coming in and bad things going out.

*Gauge for yourself the scale of your emotion – this assists in behaving appropriately for the level of feeling you're having. If you scale the happy feeling 0=ok and might be at just waking up in the morning. Being with your family might be at a 5=great and going to Disneyland might be a 9 or 10=amazing/ecstatic. In this scale example it would be more appropriate to scream and dance with the news of a trip to Disneyland but would be a bit extreme for simply waking up to a new day.

*List of Emotions – it is helpful to grow our vocabulary of feelings as we get more in the habit of expressing them in healthy ways.

Set the example and describe your emotions to those around you. Have conversations with your kids such as, oh that would be hard, what do you think that kid is feeling after the boy said that? Identifying and recognizing emotions in other people is a valuable skill as well. We learn so much in observing and copying.

Relax Tools including graphics for use with Children

If you are a parent helping a distressed child, check out my website http://www.joyhitztaler.com I created a PowerPoint geared for kids, it is under the "Resources" link, titled "Relax Tools". I also have a few games for purchase on my website that involve these Relax Tools.

I am including a similar version as my PowerPoint here. Also, on my website I have a video of myself giving a description of all the Relax Tools, it is nearly 20 minutes long. Meanwhile, here are some tools for you to help your child through a stressful time.

Practice these tools daily to be able to employ them when needed, when upset, mad, sad, lonely, hurting etc.

**Take deep, slow breaths

1…..2…..3…..4…..5…...6…..7…..8…..9…..10…..

**Blow bubbles

**Be like a turtle, take some time to yourself

**Do some exercise! It helps use up some of the extra adrenaline & energy.

**Play a game, do a puzzle.

**Visualize your favorite place, person, or activity.

**Find Scripture that applies to your heart & feelings.

When I'm worried," Cast your cares on Jesus, for He cares for you." I Peter 5:7

**Pray, meditate

**Talk with someone--your mom, dad, brother, sister, friend, pet.

**Have something to drink. It helps your body go into auto-pilot breathing.

**What ideas do you have?? (hint: any activity you enjoy)

**Be like a raw noodle, then cooked noodle. Flex and relax your muscles.

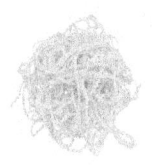

**Write or draw what you are feeling. Some people like to put it in a box or rip it up. Coloring books are relaxing too.

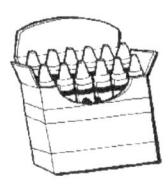

**Read some jokes or watch something funny.

**Read – a book, magazine, the internet

**Watch a show you like.

**Try to help someone else.

**Pop a balloon or rip up some paper.

**Shake the dog or do the wiggle.

**Squeeze a stress ball, or something else.

**Sing or listen to music.

**Take a nap.

**Take a shower or bath.

**Consider changing your thoughts.

**Tell your thoughts or worries to leave.

**Breathe in the good, breathe out the bad.

**Gage for yourself the scale of the emotion. i.e. 0= sad…5= real sad….10= super-duper horribly sad

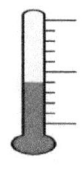

List of emotions

Happy – fulfilled, content, glad, satisfied, optimistic, pleased

Excited – ecstatic, energetic, aroused, bouncy, nervous, perky, antsy

Tender – intimate, loving, warm-hearted, sympathetic, touched, kind, soft

Scared – tense, nervous, anxious, jittery, frightened, panic-stricken, terrified

Angry – irritated, resentful, miffed, upset, mad, furious, raging

Sad – down, blue, mopey, grieved, dejected, depressed, heartbroken

*all clip art from PowerPoint free clip art gallery and Canva

Appendix II Journal Prompts and Writing Space for you to Express your Thoughts

***Journal prompt 1: What is the story of your loved one? What kind of person were they? What did they stand for? What are some memories you have of them and with them? What emotions did you have shortly following their passing? What emotions (if applicable) have you been having as time passes?

***Journal Prompt 2: What ideas do you have for activities to do in memory of your loved one? What were they into? What did they enjoy doing? Food they liked? Music? Any things you enjoyed together? It can be hard to do things without your loved one, think how they would be happy you continued to enjoy what you once did together.

***Journal Prompt 3: What are your thoughts on a higher power? God? The universe? What part of your life does your higher power have? Do you pray or talk to God? Do you make decisions by the values connected to your beliefs? Do you mediate? Do you practice affirmation or mantras?

***Journal Prompt 4: What impact has your debilitating thought life and related emotions had in your life? What have you gained as a result of your thought patterns?

***Journal Prompt 5: What emotions do you recognize in yourself as you grieve your loved one? What does it mean for you to have these emotions; do you believe something about yourself as a result? Do you notice some emotions that were present right away and others that came with the passing of time? What emotions do you think other people expect from you? Have you been surprised by emotions you've had surrounding the death of your loved one to suicide? Do you feel bad about any of the emotions you have felt? Are you confused as to why you would feel the way you have? Some people are quick to label what they're feeling to be able to let others know how they are doing. This can be limiting. Take the time to consider the various emotions that are common to grieving.

***Journal Prompt 6

What Relax Tools do you think you use or would like to try? What do you enjoy doing? What activity can you do while being intentional to relax, calm down, center yourself? Remember to be thankful for this time, appreciative of your body and how you can have control.

***Journal Prompt 7

What have you found helpful, healing, or life-giving in the time since you lost a loved one?

***Journal Prompt 8

What have you learned in the grieving process? About yourself? About others? About loss and grieving? About life?

***Journal Prompt 9

Have you been able to help others as a result of your experience?

Who are you going to help now? Does anyone come to mind? This may seem or feel like an overwhelming question, just give it some time to sink in. Give yourself time to process through, grow and heal yourself. And at some point, I believe you will be ready to share and help others who have lost loved ones. As a natural progression we work inward and grow to the point of working outward – helping others.

Resources

• **http://www.joyhitztaler.com** is my website. Under the "Resources" Link you'll find the Power point called "Relax Tools", scanned notes from Parenting classes, as well as other helpful information.

• For teenagers/students

> • School counselors – many schools offer individual meetings as well as groups for various difficulties. A counselor can be asked to check in on a student of concern.

> • Pastor, youth leader, teacher, coach – if your child looks up to, respects, loves an adult, then they can be a valuable resource for conversation. Sometimes kids don't want to talk to their parent about everything. Most important is that they talk to someone, and trusted adults around you can be valuable relationships.

> • Teenage Suicide Prevention

>> - http://www.teensuicide.us/articles3.html

> • Teen Suicide Statistics -- http://teensuicidestatistics.com/

• American Foundation for Suicide Prevention -- https://afsp.org/campaigns/national-suicide-prevention-week-2017/?utm_source=All+Subscribers&utm_campaign=8262322599-nspw_17&utm_medium=email&utm_term=0_3fbf9113af-8262322599-382284269

• National Suicide Prevention Lifeline Phone Number: 1-800-273-8255

• Suicide Prevention Resource Center -- http://www.sprc.org/

• American Association of Suicidology -- http://www.suicidology.org/suicide-survivors/suicide-loss-survivors/suicide-support-groups

- Online Crisis Chat Suicide Prevention Lifeline --
https://chat.suicidepreventionlifeline.org/GetHelp/LifelineChat.aspx

- Online Crisis Chat Suicide Prevention Lifeline --
https://chat.suicidepreventionlifeline.org/GetHelp/LifelineChat.aspx

- http://www.suicidology.org/suicide-survivors/suicide-loss-survivors/suicide-support-groups

- http://www.sprc.org/effective-prevention/comprehensive-a

Additional Resources by Joy Hitztaler

- What Now? Anxiety, Depression, & Grief: A Concise Guide, Tools for Adults and Children
  Available in paperback and e-book $5.97 and $1.99 current pricing

What Now? Book is available on Amazon & my website; the other games are available on my website: http://www.joyhitztaler.com/shop

- Relax Tools Flash Card Game. Laminated.

- It's Your Choice – Make it Good board game utilizing Relax Tools for Children. Laminated.

- Relax Tools One Page & Half Page pictures only reference

card - for your refrigerator, backpack, purse etc. Laminated.

- Relax Tools 97c booklet – PDF printable color and fill out small workbook for kids.

About the Author

Joy Hitztaler lives in Enumclaw, WA with her husband of 13 years, along with their three young children. She received her BA in Psychology from Northwest University as well as her MA in Counseling Psychology at Northwest University in Kirkland, WA. She is a licensed Mental Health Counselor (LMHC) since 2007. She works part-time at her private practice downtown Enumclaw, counseling children, families and individuals. She is involved at a local church with her kids. Joy loves being with her family and friends, playing outside, hiking, camping, running, baking, reading, creating, sewing, and learning.

Please write a review on Amazon; it enables me to help more people as it makes my work more visible and readers trust others' recommendations!

Visit my webpage for other resources and information

http:///www.joyhitztaler.com and e-mail questions or comments to joy@joyhitztaler.com

CPSIA information can be obtained
at www.ICGtesting.com
Printed in the USA
LVHW040122050919
629995LV00019B/1737/P